<u>Social Security Redefined:</u>

Adding Health Care Reform

While

Giving the Consumer Choice and Control

Jim Thompson

2nd Edition April, 2010

Table of Contents

Foreword

A Better Way

There are millions of uninsured Americans. This is because of current health care funding, not lack of availability. The fact that there are millions of Americans without health insurance drives up the costs for those who are insured. Therefore, the concept of mandating health care for all and funding it appropriately makes both economic and ethical sense.

This document seeks to provide an effective, affordable, and relatively simple solution that will benefit every individual American, the public at large, employers, and the providers of health care. But it goes much further. When the funding issue is addressed through the means discussed in this book, it will become clear that more can be done to address all of the basic financial rights that Americans could, or should have. Doing so can eliminate waste, administrative costs, overlap, and redundancies.

While the funding methodology is addressed here, the healthcare delivery component—the providers of care: hospitals, doctors, clinics, etc.—are not, as the two are, and should be, separate. When the funding issue is resolved, much of the delivery component will react positively and benefit from it in several ways that will also benefit consumers and the nation as a whole.

As government seeks ways to reform health care, what will most likely occur is another "Band-aid" solution of the type that has been used in the past. Once the following concept is understood, it will be evident that current programs such as Social Security, Workers Compensation, Medicare, and Medicaid have all been Band-aid solutions. While they have all been valuable and necessary in many respects, overlap, over-insurance, redundancies, inequities, and bureaucracies have resulted, at great cost. All of the benefits provided by these programs and more can be simplified and incorporated into one newly defined and designed Social Security program.

Let's step back, look at the big picture, question everything, and ask: Is there a better way? If we were to start all over again, knowing what we know now, could a better system be created? Can the inequalities that exist in their present forms, which inhibit the delivery of health care to those that need it, be rectified? Can coverage be mandated and funded on a consistent, fair, and equal basis to all, including those on the lowest rung of the economic ladder? Can choice and control be given to all? Can we foster creativity and free-market competition at the same time? Can checks and balances, including advocates for the consumer and proper government regulation, be built in to the system? And can an entirely new single system be created that effectively provides for basic financial security for all Americans?

Yes.

Social Security Redefined

The title of this book, *Redefining Social Security,* is better understood after we first define the term *Social Security* and what it *should* mean. Many American have come to expect limited, but valuable, benefits from Social Security. But should Social Security be limited to the few benefits it now provides? If we were to look at Social Security as a basic platform for providing essential and basic financial security for all Americans, should it then be limited to what was created years ago to satisfy a limited definition? Or could it be expanded to cover all of the basic financial securities that should and can be provided to all Americans? If Social Security indeed provided for all of the basic financial necessities for every American, the economy would be stronger for it. If it could be changed to eliminate redundancies, overlap, and confusion; while also reducing costs, I propose that it should be considered.

Social Security is the name the government applied to a program that was established in 1935 that in reality only provided the citizens of this country with limited security. Limited, because it only dealt with specific problems the government wanted to rectify at that time. Along with its limitations, it was never funded properly, which is why there has been so much talk of Social Security going broke or not being able to survive long enough for the baby boom generation to realize its goals.

The current version of Social Security is indeed very limited in its scope. It is limited to only a few benefits—needed benefits, but limited nonetheless. This is not to say what was created wasn't necessary or that it should be discarded. In essence, a paradigm shift is needed within the psyche of the American public to consider, and hopefully embrace, a change that will substantially increase Social Security and that could include many other benefits, including:

- National health care reform
- Retirement savings
- College savings
- Survivors benefits
- Disability insurance (SSI Reform)
- Long-term care insurance
- Unemployment insurance
- Dental insurance
- Vision insurance
- Individual choice
- Free-market competition among providers

America and Americans have come to define Social Security benefits as their retirement plan. It was never meant to be. It was meant to be a very basic program that would keep people from poverty after retirement. But for many Americans, it *is* their sole retirement plan. They have no other retirement plan, because they feel this will provide adequate security for them during retirement.

There are other Social Security benefits as well, namely survivors benefits and disability benefits. Again, these were only meant as back-up plans to keep affected people from poverty.

In another context, true social security would also mean that American society should be free of worry about physical safety, including invasion by other countries, crime, and other potentials for physical harm. For the sake of this argument, however, we will focus on the financial aspects of funding health care and retirement.

Social security then, in its purest sense, should mean the security of knowing, through the guarantees put forth in the system, that as American citizens, we will have access to and funding not only for our retirement, but for our financial health as well. It should—and, I argue, can— become a system whereby we are free from worry that our finances will be wiped out due to a costly medical condition. We should also be free of the current anxiety and questions as to whether Social Security will be solvent when we need it most. We should also be secure in knowing that the funds we are putting into the system for our own good at a later time will be there for our benefit when we need them.

Beyond Social Security, we also need to question other federal programs. If all health-related items were taken care of within the new system proposed in these pages, there would be no need for Medicare, Medicaid, employer-sponsored health insurance, or even the insurance component of Workers Compensation.

Social Security was first signed into law in 1935. Medicare and Medicaid were signed into law in 1965 as amendments to Social Security. The initial Social Security law was designed mainly to give assurances to society that the elderly need not live out their years in poverty. The poverty rate among the elderly prior to the act was over 50 percent. Medicare and Medicaid dealt with the funding of health care for the poor and the elderly. In 2010, the government is trying to come up with an entirely separate program that will deal with health coverage for all Americans. Current proposals would leave intact the overlapping, Band-aid solutions of the past, and add a new program: one that will again create overlap, over-insurance, redundancies, and far too much administrative cost, as well as more bureaucracies to oversee it all.

I chose the title *Redefining Social Security* for a few reasons. Number one, Social Security is a term that every American is familiar with. Secondly, the proposed redefinition would provide for current and future benefit expectations that must be guaranteed as a right to those who are expecting them and would be required to be incorporated into any replacement program. Third, the current mechanics of funding Social Security are a natural model for the funding of the proposal included within this document. The existing funding relationship—collecting Social Security taxes using employer-based deductions from paychecks and self-employed tax contributions—can and should be used as the funding model for the proposed change. The system is already in place. It works.

The flaw that needs to be redefined is not how money is collected, but how it is paid out. When Social Security was first passed, and as it stands now, the funds going in are immediately disbursed to those receiving the benefits. This is fine; so long as you have more people putting in than there are collecting. This demographic is changing, however, and will become a real problem for the baby boomer generation. Already, amendments have been made to encourage people to retire later, using higher payouts as an incentive.

The Plan

The plan as outlined here is conceptual; it lays the foundation for the system, yet doesn't entirely define the dollar amounts, nor every nuance and detail that will eventually be incorporated into the plan. Although the concept is simple, some of the details are not, and they will need to be identified, debated, and negotiated and planned for before the final version is formalized. While the concept is what is being proposed, I am also proposing that through debate and consensus, these details can be worked out, leaving the majority of the concept intact. As the concept itself is realized and people's paradigms begin to shift and change with acceptance, the details will be ironed out based on the same paradigm shift. The plan also accounts for and can accommodate changes to the details on an ongoing basis.

The Plan Defined

- Every American receives a tax rebate, annually, for the mandatory purchase of minimum benefits within the plan.

- Annually, every American chooses the benefits (with minimums and maximums) that best fit their individual needs

- The IRS will still be responsible for the collection of taxes (as they are now), but the agency will also serve as the Third Party Administrator, responsible for:
  1. Receiving taxes from employees, employers, and self-employed
  2. Sending the monies allocated by individual Americans to the organizations that were selected by those individuals for the purchase of mandated benefits.

Those are the quite simple basics. Many readers will have specific questions , and answers to most anticipated queries are included within this writing. The questions not addressed within this document can be worked out within the parameters of the principles that encompass the concept.

Some of the details and assumptions in implementing this change include:

- **Every American should be filing taxes**
  I would assume most American agree with this statement. Within the context of this plan, the filing of taxes makes the tax rebate available and usable. There would be no reason *not* to file taxes, especially with this in mind. Additionally, the filing of taxes is paramount to the plan and identifying who is to receive the tax credit and the benefits that come with it.

- **Every American will receive a tax rebate**
  Each individual will be allocated their own separate tax rebate (with parents/guardians making choices for children). The rebate will be the same for every American, regardless of age (although with debate and agreement, this might be changed to age-based amounts).
- **Every American will have to make choices about benefits**
  Although many do this already, this will universally be done individually, based on a person's individual and family needs. The technology available today can accommodate this using the Internet and the many software programs that private industry has already been using and perfecting. What will need to be addressed is the education of each person to help them make decisions on the best plans for them and their family. This is a good thing. One of the detriments of the current health care system is that the general public is not as informed as they should be about the cost of health care. This plan will ultimately change that, making every American taxpayer (now an *informed health care consumer*) more educated about health care costs, options, and cost saving principles.
- **Every financial institution and insurance carrier will have to be approved and regulated and agree to pay into an insurance pool**
  The approval process and payment into the pool will be at the federal level. The regulation of companies can remain as it is (with state regulators) or could be accomplished at the federal level. The pool will be set

up to protect the entire system and will serve as a safety net should any company within the system fail, so that individuals are protected. The companies and carriers approved may be national regional, or state-specific in scope.

- **The IRS is uniquely qualified to be the Third-Party Administrator for the plan:**
  The IRS is already set up for the collection of taxes. Administering the plan can be a simple process for them. The only additional service required of them will be the redistribution process that will allow for the payment of allocated benefit dollars to the organizations and institutions selected by each consumer.
- **The plan must and will accommodate those Americans already receiving benefits from Social Security, Medicare, Medicaid, and other government entitlement programs:**
  Current recipients can (and must) be accommodated under the plan. This can be accomplished in a few ways. But remember: These recipients will be filing taxes, getting the tax rebate; and selecting providers and financial institutions for the payment of their benefits. One idea is to have the pool fund a system to continue paying out existing benefits, until all are off the program (this attrition approach would take some time). This proposal recommends selecting or delegating contributing institutions that would take over the disbursement of those existing benefits. This could be one or several institutions, either mandated or selected by the regulators or be selected by the actual

individuals or recipients, which this proposal recommends.

- **A "Public Option" can be accommodated (though I do not recommend one)**
  I am of the opinion that, given free-market enterprise, competition within the plan will foster creativity and cost-saving measures among the various approved institutions and carriers within the plan. That being said, if the public option—a government-run competitor—is still wanted by the public and/or our representatives, it can be accommodated under the plan. Certainly this would have to be accomplished without subsidizing such an option, either through taxes, lower payments to providers, or through the use of the pool money. Additionally, a public retirement option, either as a stand-alone retirement plan or as a supplement under the existing Social Security retirement benefit, should be allowable for individuals to keep. Certainly, the individual would have to consider all the alternatives within a new system, and the social security system would have to make available a competitive product.

While some issues are addressed here, more will arise that can be addressed through the basics of the concept. The entire plan rests on the simplicity of the concept, the inclusion of all Americans, and the freedom of choice, with the government acting as facilitator and regulator and including the inherent positives that free market enterprise will bring.

The plan resolves many issues that both left- and right-wing political parties would like to address. Compromise will still be needed from both spectrums.

Employer-Based Health Insurance

The plan identifies and outlines a system that eliminates the need for employer-based health care. Although this is the current paradigm, we should question why we have an employer-based system, whether it is working adequately, and explore whether there is a better way to provide health benefits.

Employer-based health insurance has become an expected employee benefit and is the way most Americans acquire health insurance. In the past, when average Americans expected to work for the same employer, in the same location, for the majority of their lives, this was an appropriate funding method.

Employer-based health insurance has become an expectation, but it was never a plan, let alone The Plan. Employers started offering health insurance to employees after World War II to help attract employees during an improving economic climate. Once some companies began offering this benefit, other companies started to as well, to compete for employees. But it didn't begin as a deliberate plan.

Although it can be argued that for the majority of Americans—especially those with employer-funded health care benefits—the employer-based model is already working well. Conversely, it can also be argued that for too many Americans—primarily those without an employer who contributes toward health care—it is not working, which is the reason behind the massive push for health reform in 2010.

Benefits also differ from one employer to the next. Though there are some similarities, levels of benefits from one employer to the next can vary greatly. The dollar amounts employees are expected to absorb vary greatly as well. This variation creates obvious inequities from one employer to the next, from one American to the next.

Employees who are lucky enough to work for large companies or have public jobs have some of the best health benefits available. The employer typically funds a great amount of the cost of the insurance (if not all of it), and the remainder of the cost is deducted from the employee's pay.

However, times have changed. People don't typically spend their entire working life with one employer any more. In fact, most don't. Some employers have opted to hire more part-time or per diem employees, thus relieving themselves of the responsibility for providing those costly benefits. Many individuals are working two or more part-time jobs to make ends meet financially, but they lack health coverage because they don't have an employer-funded option.

Within an employer-based health care system, the self-employed are on their own. Although they may be pursuing the American dream, health insurance options for them depend on the state they live in and the options that are available in that state; they pay the full cost for their choice. While some who are self-employed do research and get health insurance policies on their own, many do not. Many look at their options and decide to assume the risk on their own. Many can't see spending hundreds (if not thousands) per month on health coverage when they are healthy. They just don't see the benefit.

And those who are unemployed or can't work due to a disability don't have an employer to fund their health insurance. Their choices (if you can call them choices) are limited to Medicare and Medicaid—or none at all.

The amount that employers spend to administer health insurance for the sake of their employees is substantial, on top of the premiums. Consider the human resources and benefits departments and all the costs associated with them. Eliminating not only the premiums but the costs associated with administration would allow employers to focus on their own businesses, rather than the business of providing health insurance for their employees. They would immediately see a decrease in the cost of doing business, allowing them to be more profitable.

If employers were no longer funding the costs of healthcare benefits and their related costs, they would save a great deal of money, maybe enough to hire more employees. Other Americans who have always dreamed of starting and owning their own businesses would be able to do so without being hindered by this outdated expectation. Eliminating the health care responsibility from employers would add fuel to America's economic engine.

The employer-based model for providing health insurance obviously has flaws. The system is outdated and no longer serves the purpose that created it some time ago. Can we in America meet this need better? Yes, we can.

Combining Many Benefits under a New Social Security

Other equally important, necessary benefits should be included within the parameters of this new concept. If not now, they will eventually become the next major reform on the agenda.

Social Security benefits as it stands now, provides for retirement benefits, disability benefits, survivor benefits, and a death benefit of $225.00. Under the new plan, all of these benefits would be replaced with individual insurance benefits. The plan would provide at least the same amount of benefits, and most likely more. Separating and discussing each may help to provide clarity.

Retirement benefits provided now under the current Social Security model are based on earnings in previous years and the age at which one starts collecting. The higher the earnings, the higher the benefit (with minimums and maximums). The later in life one starts to collect on these benefits, the higher the benefit will be (and the more likely one will die sooner and not receive full-term benefits).

The argument against the privatization of Social Security has typically centered on the unknowns regarding the quality and stability of investment vehicles. Opponents of privatization argue that Social Security will always be there, but if funds are secured in some private investment vehicle, individuals could lose everything. However, safe, guaranteed, low-interest investment vehicles are available in the open market. Annuities are among the safest long-term vehicles, while CDs and some bonds can provide guaranteed interest within stable organizations. Coupled with mandates that approved companies within the new plan would only offer products that provide guaranteed minimum interest, along with an internal "insolvency pool" (in case an approved company failed), the benefits to the consumer can be as safe as they are now and provide more choice—and even greater potential benefits.

I say "greater benefits" because someone (the named insured, or a beneficiary/survivor) will always be guaranteed to collect what has been funded within the plan. Under the current model, retirement benefits end when a retiree dies. For example, if a retiree dies at age 66 after starting to collect at age 65 and has no spouse or other dependent children (unlikely at that age), the benefits stop. The individual has paid Social Security taxes for the better part of 45 years, collected for one year, and then the benefits stop. There is very little "return on investment." If those taxes had funded an individual retirement account, the funds left over that had not been collected (whether or not benefits had started to pay out) would be available to a beneficiary. Certainly, in the example provided, the remaining benefits would be greater under a private plan than under the current model.

The current Social Security model was never organized to base individual payout on expected longevity. It was never designed to account for taxpayers on an individual basis. There was no "return on investment" planned in. It was not designed with the same principles and underwriting that an insurance company or investment firm would use. Companies that market annuities under a new plan, for example, would use a CSO Mortality schedule, which would determine (based on statistical years) the life expectancy of that individual, how long funds would be expected to be paid into, and for how long they may be paid out. Under this model, companies are able to do this with guarantees, provide a competitive plan, and still make a profit.

The current Social Security model did not implement the same principles, underwriting, and accounting methodologies that insurance companies use, and this is precisely the reason that many people worry that Social Security will go broke before they receive their retirement benefits. And they have a good point. Because Social Security was a Band-aid solution at the time it was established, the government just started taking tax money from those that were earning money and then paid it out immediately to those who were in retirement, so they would avoid living their retirement years in poverty. While that may have solved the immediate problem, it never took into account that years later we would have fewer people paying in, and more collecting. The individualization of plans within this proposal of Social Security would solve that problem, provide a "return on investment," and provide more benefits to the people.

Several retirement choices could be built into each citizen's plan, which could include a long-term, guaranteed annuity as a base, a Health Savings Account, followed by more risky vehicles with higher potential earnings. Parameters would have to be put in place to ensure that citizens first have an adequate guaranteed base before investing in any higher-risk programs. And, all high-risk programs would still provide for guaranteed minimum interest accumulation – no one would lose money.

The disability benefits provided under Social Security have very stringent collection qualifications, and the benefit amounts are not very high. It was designed to protect those in severe disability situations. If the nation were to approve National Health Care Reform as another Band-aid solution, the next Band-aid solution will probably be National Disability Reform.

Disability insurance could arguably be defined as the most important insurance individuals should have. It protects their most important asset: the ability to earn. Remove the ability to earn, and what else can be afforded? Although it is imperative that disability benefits be included under the new Social Security plan, the options for coverage have to be increased to adequately protect people.

Most people do not realize the full impact that disabilities have on individuals, as well as the entire economy. At the same time that the real estate market has gone bust over the past few years, many people are facing foreclosures on their homes. While it is in the news all the time, many have the impression that most home foreclosures are due to high-risk, adjustable mortgages or to people losing their jobs and no longer being able to afford the mortgage. While those numbers have been rising, they don't tell the entire story of mortgage foreclosures.

Historically, more than 50 percent of all mortgage foreclosures are due to a disability. This statistic has been somewhat static for years, yet why is there not the same outrage that the high-risk mortgage foreclosures have created? Being that Social Security has a disability component, why are there such high numbers of foreclosures? Although solutions have been available in the private market, and many employers provide some form of disability coverage, few individuals pursue the protection that is available. It only makes sense that this will be the next reform initiative.

The new Social Security proposal will enable citizens to shop for and customize a disability program that fits their needs better than the present system. It will remove the employer from the equation and mandate coverage for all citizens. With adequate coverage in place, the entire economy will benefit from fewer home foreclosures. People with disabilities and their families will not have to suffer the emotional and sociological ramifications of foreclosure, moving, and changes in lifestyles.

The choices citizens will be able to make will give them the ability to design programs that fit their individual needs and wants. For example, when the savings within a retirement account are substantial enough, an insured can increase the waiting period (the time after a disability one must wait before receiving benefits) and therefore save premiums toward their disability program, which in turn could serve to increase their retirement savings.

The final, major part of the current Social Security model is survivors' benefits. These are benefits that are available should a current taxpayer die or become disabled, leaving survivors or other family members who are dependent upon them.

Let's briefly review how survivor's benefits will improve with the new proposal regarding both retirement benefits and disability benefits: First, as individual retirement benefits are accumulated through contributions, the dependents or beneficiaries will stand to benefit. With a much-improved disability program, the loss of income will not be nearly as great as might be expected under the current system.

In the current Social Security model, there is a $225 death benefit. That is easy enough to replicate through life insurance. The other survivor's benefits included in the current model—those benefits that are paid out after the death of the taxpayer—are currently paid on a monthly basis, calculated based on previous earnings and how many dependent survivors there are. The benefits are paid out while there is a surviving spouse and are increased for each surviving child. However, a limited timeframe exists when dependent children are eligible to receive these benefits.

These survivors' benefits can also be easily and cost-effectively replaced with life insurance. Again, with a multitude of choices from competing, approved providers, each citizen will be able to best plan for his or her survivors and beneficiaries. When citizens are young and single, they may start with a simple, permanent plan that doesn't increase in premium. When they start a family, they will be able to add to it, or replace it with level term insurance. When they are older and need less coverage, they can cut back. The flexibility will be built in to the system. At an older age, the savings from cutting back on life insurance will be able to go towards the higher cost of health insurance, or into a Health savings account.

This sums up the current coverage and how each would be replaced under the new plan. In addition, other coverage would be made available, including health, dental, and vision care, medical savings accounts, prescription coverage and medical discount (networks) programs. Health savings accounts were mentioned earlier because this is an important component to the building blocks of the plan. And, as mentioned, advantages would include the ability to afford higher deductible health plans and longer waiting periods on disability insurance. Other benefits would include the ability to opt out of dental, vision, or prescription coverage if there is enough of a balance to cover expected expenses should coverage be needed.

A side-by-side comparison of coverage's under the old plan, and the proposed plan:

Old	New
Retirement	Retirement
Disability	Disability
Survivors Benefits	Survivors Benefits (life ins.)
	Health insurance
	Long-term care insurance
	Dental insurance
	Vision insurance
	Health Savings Accounts
	Prescription coverage
	Unemployment insurance
	Provider Discount Networks
	College Savings Plan

To reiterate, all of the new coverage would have several options or levels of benefits to choose from. Parameters would be set up to ensure there is adequate coverage or savings at one level before allowing more lenient coverage or levels of benefits.

Marketing Insurance/Retirement Options:

In the 1980s, the government mandated the break-up of a national monopoly: the phone company, AT&T. Everyone with a land-line phone number needed to make a choice about who their long-distance carrier would now be. Marketing materials were sent out, and choices of long-distance carriers were offered. If someone neglected to make a choice of their own, one was made for them randomly from approved carriers. What seems like a simple thing now was hard for a lot of people to go through when it occurred. Why? Their paradigm was that they always had it one way: they didn't need to choose, they didn't know how to compare and choose, and so on. At the time, it seemed more complicated than it actually was.

I bring up this scenario because I believe there are, and will be, similarities with this proposed paradigm shift. With the technology available today, the type of massive change being offered can be accomplished. In the end, the majority of the public will find that they appreciate having choices to make, will be able to make them easily, and will be happier with the outcome.

Today, for the majority of Americans, health care choices are made for them by their employers. Some employers may offer a choice of carriers (a cafeteria plan), but even those choices are limited based on the size of the employer and the participation considerations, as well as the number of insurance carriers approved in the given state. Each year employers receive renewal rates from their existing carrier, as well as rates and differing plans from competing carriers. Many employers utilize independent brokers and consultants in making the decisions they make for the new plan year.

For many employers, the costs associated with their health insurance will dictate how much (if any) other benefits, like life and disability insurance, will be offered to employees within their group. Due to the ever-increasing costs, many employers have been cutting back on those ancillary benefits. In fact, many employers have started to eliminate offering health insurance altogether.

Because most Americans currently get their health benefits through their employers, the average employee is not very involved (if at all) in the decision-making process. Most employees do not know what the total cost of their health insurance premium is, but they know when their contribution rate goes up or their co-pay increases. When employees have been given some choices under cafeteria-style plans, they become more informed about the choices and individually make choices that benefit them and their family, whether through lower-priced premiums, a better carrier, or better benefits that suit their specific needs. The successful implementation of cafeteria-type plans has shown that, when given the choice, employees can and will make sound choices.

For those Americans who do not have employer-sponsored health insurance, the situation is different. As they don't have an employer making the choice for them or giving them options to choose from, the entire research and decision-making process is totally up to them. They need to research the various carriers approved in the state, the various options available, and the costs, and then make choices. And of course, the entire premium is up to them to pay.

The costs of health insurance for individuals (or the self-employed) can be enormous. Even when comparing individual premiums against employer-sponsored premiums, the costs can be significantly higher for individuals and the self-employed. There also may be more stringent underwriting for an individual than for employer-sponsored plans. Although variations exist by state, pre-existing conditions may result in limitations to coverage (if they are covered at all), and coverage can be denied outright in some cases for individual or self-employed plans.

Beyond health insurance, many employers offer or provide retirement benefits. Social Security (as it is now) provides for some retirement benefits as well. Many large employers in the past provided defined benefit plans, where the benefit received in the future would be defined as a percentage of and a guarantee of future retirement benefits, qualified by how many vested years one had (based on longevity of service to that employer). These plans have been cut back over the years, due to their increased costs and a more mobile employment generation.

Defined contribution plans have increased over the past few decades; they help to more clearly define, based on contributions from the employer, what the employer costs will amount to. They are more easily planned and accounted for, and they cater to the mobile work force as well. Matching contributions to 401k and 403b plans have also gained in popularity, and employers can help by matching contributions as well. With many of these plans, especially those that provide matching contributions, group and individual education and employee enrollment are required. As it is extremely important for employees to understand what these plans have to offer, what the employer is making available, and the potential benefits to each employee, enrollment in these products currently mandates significant face time with employees.

With technology, that face time can be minimized through Web-based education and video and phone conferencing to save time and expense involved in the delivery of the products to the consumer. Many financial institutions and insurance companies make available a range of different enrollment methodologies to not only enhance the education process but also to gain more customers by providing the best systems and products possible.

With this in mind, under the new plan many different marketing and enrollment methodologies can be accommodated. It will be up to the financial institutions and insurance carriers to market, educate, and enroll prospective clients in the most efficient way possible to maximize potential as well as keep their expenses low.

Web-based technologies and the Internet would certainly provide for some of the most readily available and practical solutions. However, individual face-to-face services of financial planners, independent insurance brokers, and company agents may be used, or they may supplement other electronic methods.

When employer-based plans are eliminated, several things will happen. First, employers will be freed from the benefits equation. They will no longer have to spend time every year shopping, analyzing, and purchasing benefits. They will have more time to spend on their own business concerns. Many employers will eliminate or substantially cut back their employee benefits and human resources departments, possibly displacing employees in those departments.

The financial institutions and insurance carriers will have to increase their sales and marketing departments and personnel in order to provide the best sales and service to all the new prospects and customers created by the plan. And they will have to do it in a way that maximizes productivity, while keeping expenses low.

When free-market enterprise is allowed to flourish under the new plan, companies will find the best ways of providing the best products at the least cost. When they do, they will be imitated, copied, and duplicated by other companies. If they don't, they will fail, or at least not be as successful as they could be otherwise.

Individual Choice: Selection of Various Options

Some critics to this plan may insinuate that having individual Americans making their own decisions regarding their individual benefits will be difficult. They may believe this approach will be too difficult to administer; that people will neglect to do it, or that citizens don't have the capacity (understanding or know-how) to accomplish the selection process. However, with the advent and ever-increasing use of cafeteria-style plans, employees have shown they are capable, willing, and in fact appreciative of being given choices that employers make available.

Administration can be accomplished with available technology. The Web, combined with software that is either readily available now (or can be produced), can make the enrollment process achievable. The existing Internal Revenue Service and Social Security Administration already have the capability to collect taxes and administer benefits.

The proposal under this plan is in fact to make a cafeteria-style program available to *all* Americans, with no discrimination as to their employer or employment status. Although many Americans have cafeteria-style plans through their employers, many do not. Certainly for some small employers, the ability to offer cafeteria-style plans may be too difficult to implement and/or administer. The self-employed have access to many benefits, but all on their own (there is no system). The self-employed are also limited to what they, as individuals, can acquire in the market. Cafeteria-style plans cater to larger group benefits and result in lower costs.

Giving choice to every American through the new plan will not only foster creativity and cost-control with the approved companies in the plan, it will also produce more educated, involved consumers. Free-market competition will invariably foster creativity within the system, and the plan should accommodate creativity, within certain minimums or maximums that are approved and/or found to be in compliance with the standards set forth for approved vendors. Cost controls and expense controls will be necessary to stay competitive. Vendors will have to restrain their expenses to remain viable and approved, let alone competitive.

The more educated and involved the consumer, the better. Once consumers of the benefits being offered become educated about their various options, they will start to understand the benefits and consequences of making decisions. Approved companies will have to cater to a more educated and involved prospect and customer base as well. Eventually, the system will foster both educated and involved consumers and more savvy vendors catering to that more informed audience. At the heart of consumer choice will be the one of the most significant health care cost-saving mechanisms of all: an interested, educated consumer of the service who wants to save money. While there are many current and proposed plans to reduce the cost of health care, putting the consumer in charge of watching where the dollars go will have by far the biggest impact. This single point and the resulting outcome can not be overestimated when considering this proposal.

Mandates on Participating Carriers

First, there are many financial institutions and insurance carriers in existence today that will want to be approved vendors and a part of this new system. The changes they will need to make will have more to do with their marketing and distribution strategies than anything else. New companies will also emerge to participate and compete. The possibilities and opportunities for all of these companies will be massive, as they will now have willing, educated consumers who have the funding necessary to buy their products.

With inclusion as a selected vendor also come responsibilities. Those responsibilities and mandates may differ, depending on whether the vendor is a financial institution providing retirement services or an insurance carrier providing health care benefits.

The first mandate to be addressed is accommodating those individuals already collecting benefits in the system. There can not be any loss to those currently in (or about to enter) the system with respect to benefits. Retirees and the currently disabled are the best examples. But all recipients in the current system need to be accommodated and to receive at least the minimum that they are entitled to.

There are two distinct alternatives to accommodating those in the system. One would be to include everyone in the same system (the new system being proposed) and enable those individuals to choose which companies they want to handle their benefits. The second would be to leave them in the current system until those in the system exit the system through attrition. The first option, I believe, is the best. This way *all* Americans will convert to the new system.

Keep in mind that all Americans will receive a tax rebate and will have to make choices about not only which companies get their money, but also which ones they choose to service their needs and to collect the benefits from. Should the second alternative be used, the tax rebate would be negated for those already within the system. For most already collecting in the current system, this will not be a very big issue, as in all likelihood, they will be collecting more than their tax rebate would be. What will be more important is the service provided by their chosen vendor.

It can be assumed that those already collecting in the system now will create a drain (or a loss) to those companies that are chosen to disburse their benefits. With this in mind, a system or pool needs to be created to offset the losses on a fair basis to those companies that are now responsible for those individuals. Which system is initiated will determine how this pool is funded and distributed. In the first option (all Americans switch), the companies that were chosen by participants will receive pool money to offset their expected losses in a fair, balanced, per-capita way. If the second alternative is used (current system remains for existing users), the pool money could be used to fund the current benefits.

The pool will also be used to create a 'vendor failure' contingency should a vendor collapse, quit, or go into bankruptcy. State insurance departments currently have similar plans in place, and they can be used as a model. They typically charge a small percentage of all insurance premiums to protect the insurance-buying public from disaster should an insurance company fail. It is a big part of what makes insurance safe.

Another model to consider is the National Workers Compensation Insurance Pool, created to offset the potential for excessive claims against risks insurance companies would not normally cover, due the high risk exposure. It is very similar to what is being proposed here.

Dealing with active recipients within the current system and the ultimate transition to the new system is one of those details that needs to be debated, defined, and agreed upon before the transition is implemented. Under either scenario, an overall agreement with the entire concept of the new plan should be maintained. The transition is a long-term, long-range issue that will be solved over time, either way. One hundred years from now, the transition issue will be a moot point. The new system and the new plan will survive without future Band-aid reforms.

Additional mandates will apply. Each segment of the plan will have differing sets of mandates that need to be addressed for the plan to be successful. Although more will inevitably be suggested, here is a sampling of some of the necessary mandates:

Retirement Accounts

- State and other regulatory approvals: Please see Health Insurance, below.
- Minimum percentage on investments: The percentage to be used as a minimum needs to be debated and agreed upon.

Health Insurance

- *State and other regulatory approvals*: Companies have to be approved in the state by that state's Insurance Department. Should a federal regulatory agency replace the state departments, the same or similar regulations must be met, and approvals will need to be in place.
- *Guaranteed issue*: Companies will not be able to turn down applicants due to health conditions. As all Americans will now be insured, there will be less likelihood of adverse selection (the term for when a companies' risk increases due to the likelihood of insuring high-risk clients).
- *Non-cancelable* (by insurance company): Unless a company exits from the entire system (the pool will protect consumers in this instance, and consumers will be able to switch companies), they can not cancel an insured for a health condition—or any other reason, for that matter.
- *Minimum amounts of coverage*: Although a company will be able to offer a wide range of benefit offerings, minimum levels of coverage and maximum deductibles will have to be offered.

Individual Components of the Plan

Health Insurance:

It is appropriate to start with the health insurance component, as this is the greatest proposed change to the existing Social Security system, as well the best way to advance the much sought-after and necessary health care reform. Under this proposal, all Americans will be insured. The funding dilemma will be satisfied. All Americans will be able to choose their own health insurance. Employers will be alleviated of the responsibility to provide health insurance benefits.

Choice of health insurance carriers may be limited or changed regionally. This can be due to either the state insurance regulators, or based solely on the health insurance carrier and their networks. Free market competition will enable carriers and organizations to become customer-focused and will foster creativity regarding the level of benefits and extra services providers can offer.

The most obvious major changes will be the lack of employer involvement and the new individual responsibility for carrier selection. These will change how health insurance carriers market, price, package, and service policies to their prospects/clients. It will make all participants smarter about their choices, and carriers will have to educate consumers and compete on a different level than today.

Retirement/Savings

As the current Social Security plan's main focus is on retirement benefits, we will explore and consider the differences between what is and what could be. The current social security system can now be described loosely as a "Defined Benefit" system. That is, the benefit that can be expected during one's retirement is defined by a formula based on average past wages.

Under the proposed plan, Americans would pay into a "Defined Contribution" plan. The amount that goes into the retirement/savings component is pre-determined, but not the benefit. The amount going in to retirement/savings can be higher than the minimums set forth in the plan but not lower. The benefit derived from the plan (i.e.: the accumulated savings over time) will be higher or lower depending on the choices the individual makes. Those choices would include how wisely they used the rebate they received, as well as their choice of financial institution and savings vehicles. As outlined elsewhere, a minimum percentage would apply for any savings vehicle in the plan, but choosing wisely could yield higher returns.

How wisely consumers apply their tax credit can be explained in simple terms. For example, when one considers the costs associated with health insurance options, savings may be derived from using a higher deductible health plan. Assuming a greater risk for the initial health care dollars by choosing a higher deductible then generates savings that can be redirected into the retirement/savings component of the plan.

A base plan will need to be defined, based on conservative, guaranteed assumptions. In the investment world, this may be likened to bonds or annuities. As the account accumulates, additional savings vehicles (in addition to the base, safe plans) can be considered and purchased. Medical savings accounts and college savings accounts could become parts of this overall strategy as well; they will be discussed next.

The American public, which now seems to be stuck in debt and unable to save, will start saving under this arrangement. As Americans get smarter about their choices on other components within the new plan, the savings plans will begin to and continue to increase. People will want as much as possible of their tax rebate going into savings. Investment firms will prosper with newly educated customers. Investments will ultimately mean new capital going into the American economic engine, and new jobs.

Many will call this "privatization" of Social Security. And it may be. However, a public option can be included here as well. Assuming there will be no subsidizing for a public option, we can then give the choice to individuals, allowing individuals to make informed decisions after considering fair and accurate comparisons.

Health Savings Accounts (HSA)

Health savings accounts have been around since 2003. They were created as a means to set aside tax-free money in savings accounts that can also be used to pay for eligible out-of-pocket medical expenses. In order to qualify to set up one of these accounts, you also needed qualified high-deductible medical insurance.

The intent of these plans was, and still is, sound. There have been steady increases in the marketing and use of these accounts over the past several years. While they are similar (in tax status) to an Individual Retirement Account (IRA), the savings can be used to pay for eligible medical expenses. The funds roll over year to year. At retirement, the funds can be withdrawn in much the same way as an IRA. Within the new plan, they have their place as well.

The ability of an individual to choose a higher deductible health insurance plan should be predicated on the ability to pay for medical services. If consumers want a higher deductible plan, they must have savings built up within a health saving account (HSA) before they can increase their deductible. For example, if they want a health insurance plan with a $5,000 deductible, they must have at least $5,000 in their HSA. And when they have a medical procedure done, the provider must be assured of payment. If necessary, a debit-type card must be presented, giving the provider access to the consumer's account for payment of the deductible.

The major difference between a current HSA would be its tax status. Under the new proposal, funds would be made available through the tax rebate. Under the new plan, the important component is the separation of the HSA from retirement savings, and its current availability for use for medical expenses. Its current tax-favored status is replaced due to the new tax rebate.

Although funds could still be made available at retirement as they are now, individuals may choose to keep the plan going into retirement. As the new plan proposes the elimination of Medicare and Medicaid in favor of health carriers covering individuals in retirement, there may still be value in continuing an HSA.

College Savings

A tax credit will be given to *all* Americans, including the very young. While the premiums for insurance will be minimal for the young, the ability to allocate the maximum possible dollars to savings opens a wide range of possibilities. It is commonly understood that most American are not saving the way they should or could. Many live paycheck to paycheck. Many carry more debt than they should. When dollars that will be allocated to an individual at an early age are being used properly, with limited access, the savings among all Americans will grow.

Consider this: access to, and funding for, advanced education can be provided under a new Social Security.

This option is very far-reaching, but when considered in the context of this entirely new concept, it is conceivable. It could also reduce or eliminate other bureaucracies and the costs that come with them. Higher education would then be available to *all* Americans.

Similar to the concept that *all* American should have health coverage; if we apply the same thinking to college/advanced education—*all* American should have access to and funding for higher education—would the U.S. economy and standard of living be advanced? Will Americans be able to compete better on an international level with higher education participation? Will the country be better, as a whole, when higher education is advanced?

Current rules for retirement accounts and other tax-favored savings plans (401-k, 403-b, etc.) allow tax-favored treatment of withdrawals for qualified education costs. Similar qualifications and fund availabilities can, and should, be incorporated within the new plan. While those in their working years will have to follow minimum guidelines, with very limited access to the accumulated retirement dollars, the very young will have access to funds for higher education costs. In the end, as a society, we will end up with an increased population of college-educated Americans, who should be earning more and contributing more in many ways.

Survivors Benefits

Under the current Social Security program, survivors of a spouse and/or parent can expect to receive a monthly benefit. The benefit is calculated based on the wage earner's average wages, as well as age and number of dependents. The more dependents (especially children), the greater the monthly benefit.

All of the current benefits provided under this provision can be replaced with life insurance. A minimal amount will be mandated under the new plan, but individuals can choose more, as well as what kind (i.e.: term or whole life) with limitations. The main consideration is that there will be a minimum amount to replace what is in the current system.

Many Americans do not own their own life insurance. They expect that the current system will take care of them. The survivors benefits under the current Social Security model were meant to be very basic. Like the retirement benefits under Social Security, survivors benefits were meant to provide a base—a benefit that would keep survivors from poverty. Unfortunately, people have come to expect that because they have the Social Security "safety net," they will be well covered.

Often people don't own life insurance because it is not marketed to them in the same fashion it once was. It is not cost-effective anymore for insurance companies to send salesman out door-to-door to collect premiums and suggest new plans to families when changes occur. Instead, insurance companies target high-wage earners on an individual basis. Or they offer supplemental plans for employees above and beyond group term life insurance. Or they mass-market expensive plans over the television and through the mail.

Individuals who presently own their own life insurance have either considered the potential benefits their survivors could expect from the current plan or don't feel comfortable that those benefits will be there when they are needed. Either way, they chose to act on their own to secure their potential survivors by purchasing life insurance.

Under the proposed plan, individuals will have to choose for themselves whether they want minimum limits, or more. One thing I believe will happen is that more people will choose more than less, due to increased education and increased understanding of financial planning. Just allowing individuals to choose will help spur the education process, and everyone will benefit because of it.

Disability Insurance

Although we first want to make a comparison based on what is current under the existing Social Security system, there are other disability benefits available from other sources as well. Because those other systems may be impacted by the new program, we will attempt to address them all.

Before addressing these benefits, I will first offer that should a Band-aid solution be approved in the name of health care reform, the next reform issue (and next Band-aid solution) will be disability reform. The consequences of disabilities to individuals, families, and society as a whole are far-reaching.

Given the uproar over the recent sub-prime mortgage crisis, one would think that this explains why all foreclosures took place. However, nearly two thirds of all recent mortgage foreclosures are due to medical-related issues. A high percentage of those actually had medical insurance. These numbers, it could be argued, will not change should only health care reform become a reality. These foreclosures are not due as much to the lack of medical insurance or care, but the reduction in income that families experience due to the medical condition and recovery. Adequate disability insurance would alleviate this social issue.

The average American thinks their house is their biggest asset. They buy insurance for the house and cars. When a disability strikes and their income is shut off, or even cut back, all of those assets are at risk. As an analogy, take the goose that lays golden eggs. If you could only insure either the eggs or the goose's ability to lay eggs, which would you choose? The fact is that a person's ability to earn income is their biggest asset, not the assets they have bought with that income.

Most people are uninformed regarding their benefits, and many are confused, not only as to their Social Security disability benefits, but also to their employer-provided disability benefits (if any) and Workers Compensation. I have met many employees who think Workers Compensation covers them for disabilities that occur at home, or for sickness.

This is where overlap of programs and benefits can be, and are, detrimental to the system as a whole. If all individuals had 24-hour coverage for disabilities, with an adequate benefit amount, there would be no need for Workers Compensation benefits for disabilities. Instead, individuals are confused and uninformed.

Social Security benefits for disability are limited, at best. Again, this was meant to be a limited program, a "safety net." Unfortunately (again), people have come to expect Social Security to be there for them. Most are ignorant as to what Social Security disability benefits, or the qualifications to receive benefits, are. When they do receive benefits, they are usually shocked to find out how low they are.

Monthly Social Security disability benefit payment amounts are based on a calculation based on previous wages. The requirements that must be satisfied before becoming eligible are stringent. First, you don't become eligible to receive benefits until you have been disabled for five months. Next, you can't work for any company, at any job, at any wage, anywhere. The requirements are so stringent, and the process so confusing and stressful, that lawyers advertise getting disability benefits approved by Social Security as a specialty in TV ads.

Workers Compensation disability benefits can be confusing as well. They can also be difficult to collect on (but not as confusing or as difficult as Social Security). Lawyers advertise for collecting these benefits as well, if "...you've been turned down."

Disability and medical benefits for on-the-job accidents came about for a good reason. The first Workers Compensation laws were passed by states in the early 1900s. The laws were designed to protect both the employee and the employer. Employees were protected in that their medical care was covered and wages paid when they couldn't work due to an on-the-job accident. The employer, when covered by this law, was protected from law suits by the employee.

Prior to these laws being passed, when an employee had an accident on the job, he could be fired, without payment for medical care. When employees started suing the employers, a quagmire was started, which Workers Compensation settled.

The Workers Compensation law and its benefits work well as is. However, when workers have the benefits proposed under the new plan, namely 24-hour medical and disability coverage, Workers Compensation benefits as is become unnecessary.

While the current Workers Compensation law has served its purpose, the new plan would make it obsolete. This is not to say that parts of the law should not remain intact. But questions will need to be answered with the best consequences in mind. It should be assumed that an employer maintains a safe working environment for its employees. OSHA is already set up to monitor workplaces and levy fines if unsafe working environments are found. Broader responsibilities for OSHA could be envisioned within the new plan.

Under current Workers Compensation laws, employees can not sue their employers after an accident. This was in consideration for the employer insuring for medical care and lost wages. An elimination of Workers Compensation as we know it today might mean that employees would be able to sue employers again. Similar to tort reform under medical insurance as a cost-control addendum, a version of tort reform for work-related accidents should be implemented as well.

Under the new plan, there will be minimum guidelines for selecting adequate coverage. Coverage will be mandatory to extend to at least age 65, for instance. Giving the choice to individuals, and assuming that education and understanding levels increase as well, individuals will start making sound choices, and insurance carriers will begin getting creative to attract new customers.

Using a previous example, when individuals become more educated about their choices and levels of coverage, savings will result that can best be used in another way. For example, should an individual who accumulates significant savings choose a disability plan that has a longer waiting period (the length of time one must be disabled before benefits begin), savings will result. Those savings could then be redirected into the retirement/savings component of the plan. As time passes and the retirement/savings component of the public's plans increases, it will allow individuals the opportunity to accept more risk for the sake of savings.

Long-Term Care Insurance

Long-term care reform will be the next reform (after disability reform, as mentioned earlier). The ever-increasing need for long-term care insurance is evident by the laws and tax advantages that have been created to help promote its acceptance. Unfortunately, most people still don't have it, or can't afford it.

The dilemma with long-term care insurance is that when it is affordable, individuals don't see the need; when individuals recognize the need, it is most often unaffordable. Yet lawmakers and the insurance industry recognize the looming need that exists and are trying to get the public's attention.

At the same time as the baby boom generation ages, the need for medical care increases, and people are living longer. Longer lives often means needing help and care in very expensive care facilities. Long-term care insurance (although it's been around for a few decades now) is still the one of the "newest" type of insurance available. Because premiums increase with age, by the time an individual recognizes the need for such coverage, the premiums are all too often unaffordable. Recently, individuals are realizing the need for their own policies when they have to deal with an aging parent and the choices they need to make for them and how to pay for those choices become alarming and confusing.

Attempting to clarify the need for long-term care insurance to a 30-year-old, let alone a 20-year-old, is difficult. Their potential need is not yet apparent. Yet if a policy purchase were made at a young age and premiums did not increase (unless benefits did), then this extremely valuable benefit would become affordable. Having the entire American public insured for long-term care would (like health insurance) make the benefit more affordable and make choices easier for all.

Dental Insurance, Vision Insurance, Prescription Coverage, Medical Provider Discount Networks

I have lumped all the above for several reasons. First, although an individual could purchase all of these separately (and might still), insurance carriers within the new plan may package some, if not all, of these components together. Secondly (and unlike many of the other mandatory components already mentioned), these may become voluntary or supplemental within the program.

When people's retirement/savings portfolio (including health savings accounts) reach certain levels, they should have the ability to assume more risk with their tax rebate and within their savings portfolio. For example, when an individual has accumulated savings of $500,000, and has $20,000 in a health savings account, the new plan should enable him or her to "opt out" of the vision component of the plan and allocate more of the tax credit to savings.

As the American public becomes more educated about their benefits, and their choices, more people will be saving. More will understand risk, when they "risk" a portion of their savings. But savings will be sought after, and appreciated.

The premium or cost for vision coverage is relatively nominal. Even with accumulated savings and Health Savings Accounts, an individual who wears glasses may find coverage in the vision plan to be affordable and logical from a financial viewpoint. But such coverage should be discretionary to the individual.

Having a discount network for vision, dental care, and prescriptions may be sufficient. Such coverage may be included in the package that the health carrier is offering, or it could be purchased as a separate benefit. These networks will provide an individual with discounts and make services and equipment more affordable, whether coverage is insured, or whether the services are being paid for out of a health savings account.

One of the side effects to this will be aggressive marketing, which will include potential savings from insurance carriers. If carriers expect to market and sell these products to a more informed public, they will have to make the coverage logical and affordable. This will help to lower costs, and help people to save more.

Unemployment Insurance

Many may be surprised to see unemployment listed here as a benefit. As we are in the process of presenting something so new, with so much change, a paradigm shift is needed. Part of this paradigm shift will ask us to question everything. That includes unemployment insurance.

There needs to be a system to protect individuals who become unemployed. Under a fully encompassing and redesigned Social Security program, shouldn't unemployment be a component of Social Security? And, while the current system seems to be working, why have we saddled the employer with the cost—the very employer that we want to be hiring and employing workers? The employers are, in essence, being charged for the unemployed—the people not working for them. The only logic that can be attached to that is that the employer is the one where consistent and adequate funding for this can be generated.

As business owners (but few employees) know, state unemployment taxes are a cost borne by employers. It is based on a percentage of overall wages, and modifications can be made at the state level based on certain factors, such as occupations.

If unemployment and disability insurance pay an individual when they can't work, is it possible that the two can be combined into one policy? Would that be more efficient? Benefits already exist that can be purchased to protect things such as car loans should a borrower be laid off or unemployed. There must be actuarial tables available that can account for this risk.

The beneficiary of unemployment benefits is the employee (or past employee), not the employer. With this being the case, why is the cost borne by the employer? Can it be transferred to the employee?

If unemployment insurance becomes part of the fabric of social security and is paid for by the individual, the individual will want to do everything they can to avoid collecting on it. In other words, when it comes to job security the onus is put on the individual American, the taxpayer, the employee, rather than the employer. What should follow is a desire on the part of all individuals to do everything they can to get and stay employed.

In this scenario, the individual employee would be required to purchase this benefit from an insurance company, whether it is attached to a disability policy or on a stand-alone basis. The individual would be able to purchase better benefits than the required minimums (as with most of the other programs within this proposal). Policies might include attached riders that return a portion of the premium should there be no claims. And should premiums be predicated on risk on an individual basis, those individuals who have the most secure jobs and stay employed will ultimately pay less. However, it could be argued and debated that premiums should be level for all occupations.

Should unemployment become a part of this overall program, positive changes will occur. If private insurance companies take over the claim-paying process, it would eliminate the need for state unemployment offices. States can focus more of their efforts on employment versus unemployment. Employers would have one less responsibility, and one less tax. Their costs will decrease, their viability increase, and they may be able to grow their businesses, resulting in more employment.

Unemployment insurance is already a type of "social security." It is just named differently. It makes sense to include it within the overall change.

Pros and Cons

Employer-Funded Health Care Insurance versus the New Proposal

We have grown very accustomed to the employer-funded model over the past half-century. As mentioned previously, changing this is one of the major paradigm shifts, possibly the most dramatic, of this new proposal. The employer-funded model was never meant to be "The Plan," we just happened into it. This concept, while it worked in the initial stages when workers stayed with the same company for most of their working lives, has become outdated. Employees change jobs more frequently, employers have changed their benefits packages, including reducing or limiting benefits or benefits access, to decrease costs,. The self-employed, the unemployed, and the disabled are left with few options under the employer-funded method.

Insurance companies and their lobbying groups prefer the employer-funded model. They are stuck in this mold as well. They are used to the employer-funded and supported model, and they would rather not see it change. The perceived threats to the way insurers do business and to their profit models are based on the employer-supported benefits model. However, under this proposal, should a benefits insurer participate and embrace the change, there are advantages to the industry as well. First and foremost, insuring all Americans will open up the possibilities for substantial increases in sales. A plethora of potential new clients will become available who will need to have their individual concerns addressed. The companies that will prosper will be the ones that accommodate the new system, get creative with their product offerings, marketing, and distribution systems, and minimize expenses for the sake of increased volume.

Unions will have less to bargain for under the new proposal. Benefits are and have been a major part of their negotiations with employers for years. Their ability to include benefits within their bargaining proposals and agreements increases their validity among their own members. With benefits "off the table" (as they would be under the new system), the unions would have less to negotiate for their members. However, although benefits may be less of a bargaining chip, other potential uses for unions may appear. As changes are made to Workers Compensation, OSHA, and unemployment insurance, the potential need for more oversight in other areas that unions deal with will become more apparent. Issues like working conditions, safety, job security, member education, paid time off, and others will still be viable concerns for unions on behalf of their members. They could prove to be a vital part of keeping the employer in check while employers make the necessary changes and cutbacks in their benefits responsibilities, departments, and costs.

Government entities— federal and state governments and state insurance departments—should see little change (other than for their employees, like every other employer).

Obviously, changes are being proposed to some government entities that will eliminate the need for them over time, such as Medicare and Medicaid. Others, like Social Security, will see major changes. Workers will be displaced and moved around. Social Security may need more staff to oversee collection and redistribution of the funds. The private sector should grow more jobs, based on their now lower costs for employers, and insurance companies and financial institutions will require more personnel due to increased sales and service operations.

Individuals will be given the full advantage of being able to choose their own health care provider. Some will perceive this as a disadvantage, if they feel individuals can't make such decisions on their own. Individuals will need to become more educated on all the coverage choices, health and otherwise, that will become available to them. Because the new rebate will become "their" money, they will want to spend and utilize it wisely.

Hospitals, doctors, and all other providers will have to react to all of the changes in different ways. As the American public becomes more involved in the decision making, and therefore more involved in the costs, they will inevitably become more involved and educated in the actual costs of services, procedures, and operations than they are now. An educated and involved consumer may prove to be the catalyst for the majority of cost controls for the health care delivery system within this proposal.

Private versus Public Plans

As we've seen, there are many ways to accommodate both private and public plans within this proposal. Whether two options are appropriate will have to be decided through informed debate. If public plans are made available, they should be offered without the need for subsidies. Subsidies amount to unfair business practices. Unless a subsidy is provided for private firms, a subsidy should not be available to public entities. A subsidy, it could be argued, is already being provided under this proposal – to individuals in the form of a rebate.

The government needs to play some major roles within the new system. First, agencies need to devise a system within the Internal Revenue Service that accommodates both the intake of taxes (something they are doing now) and the distribution of funds that individuals allocate to the respective organizations they have chosen. A new level of responsibility for the IRS will be required.

The government must create and oversee the necessary regulations that participating organizations (insurance companies and financial institutions) will have to abide by. The government will be the advocate for the individual Americans covered. Both regulation and advocacy are necessary. The government must have a role in not only regulating and advocating, but also assume the role as protector of the American public—as it should.

The inherent problem with a public option is the lack of advocacy. If a person is covered under a publicly run medical plan set up by the same government that regulates the plan and makes decisions on treatments, who becomes the advocate for the insured? The idea that a government-run nonprofit health plan will "care" more about the individuals covered is inherently false. Although a government-run health plan may not have profits in mind, they also need to watch out for the bottom line, or they will have to tax people more (in other words, a subsidy).

When a privately-run health plan is regulated by government entities, those regulating agencies have the final say on "borderline" or "questionable" treatments and care. The regulators state what has to be covered and then approve the plan's definitions for coverage. The private company has to abide by the decision or be penalized. For most people under the employer-funded system, this is what they have now. Insurance providers have to have the details of their plans approved—what's covered, what's not. If they stray from those rules, they are penalized—something they don't want. While it becomes easy to blame the "big insurance company" for decisions the insured doesn't like, regulators approved the plan design. It should be the design of the plan that must meet approval, and it is the obligation of the insurer to adhere to the design and the regulator to back up what was approved.

When this all-encompassing new delivery system is implemented, that will be a good time to revisit approved plan designs. Based on issues that have occurred in the past regarding common complaints by the insured, the plan designs should accommodate such concerns. Gray areas, such as coverage for experimental treatments, should be debated and either excluded or included for coverage. When they are openly debated, the public will become more educated and will seek the coverage they desire within their insurance selections.

The public will play a major role. And insurance companies can react. Insurance companies may come up with amendments to cover experimental treatments or make available supplemental policies to do so. Individuals will have the final choice, whether they choose a company that offers an amendment or supplemental policy to cover experimental treatments or choose not to. When individuals, and the public as a whole, can make educated choices, then personal accountability comes in to play as to whether they choose to cover experimental treatments (at a cost) or not. When full disclosure of what is covered and what is not becomes mandatory and individuals choose their coverage options accordingly, then the responsibility will rest more with individuals and less on the insurance company and regulators that oversee them.

Responsibility for what is covered and what is not covered at present can be blamed on too many. It is easy for the public to blame "the big insurance company." Politicians blame big insurance companies for trying to make a profit on denied coverage, though politicians may be trying to position their own agenda. Lawyers blame big insurance companies to sell their services on TV all the time. But beyond insurance companies, regulators should share in the blame. Agents that represent insurance companies can be blamed. Employers who choose a certain insurance company or plan or agent can be blamed. When the individual is educated and has access to full disclosure, then "blame" will become "choice."

Liberal versus Conservative thinking

The proposal contains provisions that both ends of the political spectrum advocate. For conservatives, there is an increase in privatization, free-market enterprise, personal choice, and accountability. For liberals, there is a system that accommodates and insures *all* Americans equally, without perceived cost to the citizen. Yet, because of politics, each side of the political spectrum will raise issues with many of the ideas proposed here.

Conservatives may not like the mandate that everyone must buy into the program—that it will be "forced" on all Americans; that such a mandate is not included in the Constitution; that some Americans will receive the tax rebate even if they pay no taxes at all.

Liberals may argue that there should be only a government option for health and retirement; that benefits and the tax rebate should be weighted more to lower-income individuals; that this will disrupt or eliminate the complicated bureaucracies they have spent years developing.

Compromise should be considered.

Under this proposal, all Americans are insured. Private, free-market enterprise is allowed (and encouraged) to flourish. Employers are disencumbered of employee health care expenses. Government regulation is intact. All Americans get choice and control. Overlap, redundancies, and waste are reduced or eliminated. All of this costs less than it does now. Both parties could compromise and support this logical progression and change. For the benefit of the country and its citizens.

Miscellaneous

The vast changes suggested within will have lasting, and I believe positive effects on a range of different issues.

Personal accountability and responsibility will be enhanced and rewarded under this proposal. When individuals are expected to be responsible and accountable for making the decisions regarding their own financial security (rather than employers and government), the result will be a more informed and engaged public. The reward from a personal standpoint in making informed decisions will be better health, and increased wealth. Each person stands to benefit from their decisions, yet society as a whole stands to benefit by having a healthier population, and a society that has more wealth, individual savings, and less debt.

Along with the advantage of personal responsibility and accountability also comes the risk in poor decision making. While the funding under this proposal comes from the decision of the government to allow the individual to make choices with those funds, that government should be allowed use of those individual funds on a case by case basis, when an individual commits a crime.

Incarceration, in other words, can be paid for (in whole, or in part) from those funds given by government decree to the individual for individual use. The philosophy behind this is two-fold. First, the government allows the use of these funds to the individual, so it should be the expectation of the government that an individual should not commit a crime that costs the government money. Secondly, when an individual knows that the funds granted to them by the government are at risk, should the individual commit a crime costing the government money, the individual will be less likely to commit the crime. The expected result from this philosophy and practice should be reduced crime, reduced incarcerations, and decreased prison populations and costs.

It is my expectation that, after this proposal is initiated, that there will be less crime, should this provision be accepted. First, people will be less likely to commit a crime, knowing that there is a risk. Take for instance the individual who today wants to rob a convenience store for the possibility of getting a few hundred dollars as a reward for a successful robbery. Should this same individual know that they are putting several thousand dollars at risk by doing so (if not several hundred thousand dollars), there will be less likelihood to commit the crime and risk those funds. Secondly, it could be argued that the same individual that is going to rob the store is doing so because they need the money, will be less likely after the proposal has been in effect, and they have savings built up within their accounts. As it stands today, the same individual has little (if any) risk. If they rob successfully, they get the money. If they are unsuccessful, they go to jail, get three meals a day, all at taxpayers expense.

Unemployment should decrease, and jobs and pay should increase. Businesses will be un-burdened with the responsibility of providing and administering benefits, paying for workers compensation and unemployment taxes. They will be able to focus on running their businesses with less costs, thereby being able to grow and hire more workers. They will be competing against other businesses for workers based on the wages they pay, working conditions, vacations, and other perks (instead of for benefits). The playing field will be leveled.

Individuals, who are now paying for their own unemployment insurance, will be less likely to use that insurance, and will be more aggressive about finding a job, or jobs. They will not be penalized for holding several part-time jobs (as they are now due to lack of benefits), and doing so may be what that individual wants to do, or needs to do. When benefits are not attached to the job, it frees the individual to do many things – including part time jobs, or self employment.

Illegal aliens will not be a part of this system. Legal immigrants will start to reap the benefits of the system immediately. The proposal is only available to US citizens. This is not to say that an undocumented person should not receive care in a hospital. While they receive care, they should be expected to pay for it on their own. If they can not, this will be a loss the hospital they will define as being for the care of an illegal immigrant. Currently, the cost of care for illegal immigrants is comingled with uninsured Americans. These costs will be better documented and accounted for under the new proposal.

Abortion is, and always has been a political and social lightning rod. Under the new proposal, the cost will become a choice for the individual (assuming laws regarding abortion remain as they are). Abortion could be available under a health insurance policy as an option. Should an individual want that coverage, they can pay for it. It will be up to the insurance company whether they issue such coverage, and they should make it a point as to inform the buying public if they have the option, and how much it costs. Full disclosure on this coverage as well as other coverage must be a cornerstone of how health coverage is marketed and purchased within the new system.

ISSUES

Tort Reform

Tort reform will be only briefly addressed here. Tort reform has been touted for years as one of the key elements that should be added to any health care reform initiative. Instituting tort reform within the newly designed and redefined Social Security would serve to reduce overall costs. As the funding issue is addressed here, and the funding is largely affected by costs, it is appropriate then to include tort reform as a needed sub-component of the entire plan.

The cost of medical malpractice insurance has increased dramatically over the years due to the ever-increasing awards given to plaintiffs. Those increased awards have led to an increase in premiums that doctors, hospitals and other providers have to pay for medical malpractice insurance. Those increased insurance rates increase the cost of doing business for medical care providers—costs which then are passed on to patients, ultimately increasing health insurance costs.

Tort reform for medical malpractice suits should be undertaken to stabilize health insurance rates *after* hearings and debates on the issues have been conducted. While tort reform should be done from a framework of helping to stabilize health insurance rates, it should not negatively affect the very victims that tort laws are designed to protect and compensate.

One of the key themes of this entire concept and proposal is the philosophy and belief that the dollar amount of the proposed tax rebate—the funding vehicle for this proposal—will be identical for every individual. Likewise, in reference to tort reform involving medical malpractice, it could be argued that the dollar amount of specific malpractice judgments be the same from one individual to the next.

State versus Federal Regulation

Regulation must be involved. The concept proposed can accommodate either regulatory strategy, state or federal. The importance of regulation can not be underestimated.

The issue most affected by current regulatory systems is that of availability of products and services across state lines. While trying to give the consumer more choice and control, the current regulatory model inhibits the potential of multi-state availability. Each state insurance department is involved in the many tasks of approving insurers and policies. Each of the fifty states has developed similar but separate rules and interpretations of regulations.

While the state insurance regulatory model presents some difficulties regarding multi-state insurance sales, it also helps to protect consumers in ways a federal system may not be able to. The existence of, and workings of fifty separate state regulators, versus one has its merits. While one regulator may adequately oversee the regulation of large, national carriers, the ability for state regulators to regulate and oversee local or regionally-based carriers or organizations is increased. This could allow for more local non-profit, or community-based organizations (such as clinics) to be involved within the new system.

It is possible that a combination of a state and federal system can arise from this proposal. In addition, the regulations affecting the savings portion of the proposal are largely accomplished with federal regulation. The important part of this argument is that the proposal can accommodate either regulatory model.

States Rights versus Federal Rights and the U.S. Constitution

With any health care reform plan that imposes new rules on individuals as mandates the question of states rights versus federal rights comes into question. Because the Constitution of the United States has established guidelines on these issues, amendments should be considered to allow for such a mandate. If it is the will of the people to embrace this new social security proposal, amendments should be considered.

Without amendments, Social Security, Medicare, and Medicaid were all made into law. In essence, they have mandates that affect all citizens, and the funding is produced through taxes that all taxpayers must comply with. The argument can certainly be made that these federally mandated programs do not meet constitutional interpretations.

Many argue that federal income taxes were never authorized under the Constitution and that those taxes are illegal and should be abolished.

Assuming it is the will of the people to forward a proper and adequate mandate to include minimum basic financial rights as I've defined them under the Social Security umbrella for the good of all the people, as well as imposing funding regulations, then the will of the people should be recognized and appropriate language be built into the Constitution in the form of an amendment, if necessary.

Regional Issues

HMOs and PPOs can be limited with regard to the regional availability of providers within a certain network. Also, many localized HMOs and PPOs have been designed with regional consumers in mind. Such organizations should be encouraged under this proposal and should be able to flourish within this framework. Assuming the regulatory approach discussed previously also encourages the use of and expansion of these locally developed organizations, this proposal can accommodate them. Because every citizen will be allowed to choose their providers without being limited to what their employer is offering, these local organizations may see increased membership.

As free-market enterprise makes gains within this proposal, large national organizations will be competing with smaller organizations for members, insured's, and patients. While each will bring a different marketing strategy, more importantly, differing distribution strategies will appear for not only the purchase of their products but also the delivery of care to their patients. As is now, one of the deciding factors on whether consumers select one organization over another is whether their employer offers competing plans. Because of current participation requirements with insurance companies, it may not be feasible to offer all the options an employee (or consumer) may want. When the employer is removed from the equation and consumers are given free choice, it will be up to the competing organizations to competitively price and market their strengths against competitors in any given geographic location.

When the consumer is unrestricted by an employer's choice (if any) of health benefit packages offered to employees, the consumer will be free to choose the best option for their individual situation. In many cases, it could be likely that a local HMO or PPO will be the more logical, and hopefully more competitive, alternative to a national company.

Summary

The Numbers

This conceptual proposal would change many existing programs, both public and private. With full implementation, it is conceivable that entire departments of government could be eliminated. Insurance companies that sell workers compensation would no longer be needed. Human resource departments (or at least the benefits departments) at large companies could be reduced, if not entirely eliminated. Many of the jobs eliminated in one sector would be offset by an increase in jobs in others, especially the needed increase for marketing and servicing various plans to individuals. As marketing to individuals versus groups (employers) is more labor-intensive, more employees would be needed to fill those needs.

The amounts already being spent on the various programs outlined in this conceptual proposal are in the trillions of dollars, annually. When considering the ramifications of accepting and implementing this concept, the impact of all programs being added, as well as those being reduced or eliminated, must be considered. For example, while factoring in the increase in initial costs for medical expenses as well as disability income in covering on-the-job injuries, the resulting savings from eliminating the current costs for providing workers compensation insurance must be weighed.

When we look at the potential savings for employers in the costs of employing workers, we can also modify how employers are presently taxed. Because employers will be saving by eliminating the costs of providing health care, workers compensation, and unemployment taxes, one could envision a higher employer tax base to obtain more funds to make this program work. Most employers would welcome the idea of paying more in taxes instead of providing all the services (and covering the costs that go with them) of the programs they will be relieved of. Some employer's net difference in the cost of doing business could be lower, while some may see a net increase. That may depend on whether a particular employer was offering and funding a comprehensive benefits program.

Likewise, of the cost of health insurance as it stands now for employees will be eliminated. The amount that they are now spending, the employee's share of the cost of benefits with their employer, will disappear. It should be assumed then, that their taxes may increase as well. They are the beneficiaries of this change. They will get back in the form of a rebate what they are paying in taxes. As it stands now, in a graded income tax system, the wealthy will still pay more than the middle class or the poor. The poor may pay no taxes at all, yet still receive the rebate and the ability to choose benefits.

Not all of the programs will have a solid debit/credit, justifiable profit/loss offset to accommodate all situations. While the average medical expenditure per citizen is around $8,300/yr., we also know that certain criteria such as age and geographic location will impact numbers for any given situation.

When all is said and done regarding the numbers, the hoped-for result should be at minimum a zero-sum cost, and hopefully, a net reduction in costs. The costs of all the programs affected will not increase—but may decrease. The most important consideration is whether the concept for funding and distribution is sound. Will it accomplish what it has set out to do: provide coverage for *all* Americans?

Closing Arguments

We, as a society, have become mired in our own paradigms. We have begun to think that the only way of changing these familiar programs is through amendments, changes, and additions to already existing systems. We become so focused, with near laser precision, on one change at a time, on the current fix, that all solutions become Band-aid solutions, creating more cost, more overlap, more duplication, and more bureaucracies. We have become mired in reactive Band-aid solutions. Though they may in fact fix a given problem when implemented, they rarely fix the many other problems that still exist.

We have created systems for government, systems for employers, systems for employees, systems for the self employed. They do not always work as intended. They leave gaps and create overlap and confusion.

Why should we be bogged down with a one-fix-at-a-time solution mantra? Why have we not opened our eyes, looked around, and asked, "Is there a better way to do all of this?" Why can we not, collectively, look to the future and try to proactively address the issues that haven't yet become "problems'"? Why can we not come up with a solution that is all-inclusive, that addresses many issues under one program?

Common answers to the preceding questions can be varied, depending on your point of view. The "fix" that is needed at any particular moment becomes a rallying call for organizations, politicians, and the media. Based on an individual's own belief system, your view may be affected by those who share, or even oppose, your beliefs. But, politics may be affecting your decision as well. Those at the top of the political spectrum may have motives beyond the perceived fix. Those motives may be affecting the message.

The preceding conceptual proposal, though simple, would require changes to many existing programs. The changes required would be extensive. The way we are accustomed to now doing things would change. Our social psyche would need to change. But it can be done. This is America. We deserve a system that provides the same basic financial securities to all Americans. The tax rebates will be the same for all levels of the population: the poor, the middle class, the high-income class, as it should be. This is fair, and equitable. The basic financial securities cost the same no matter what your current standard of living is. Private investment possibilities and supplemental insurances, beyond these basic benefits, will still be available. But the basics will be covered under this newly redefined social security. The "basics" will certainly be more extensive than what exists today.

This conceptual proposal has been created without regard to politics. It mandates that everyone is to be covered under the system. That concept goes against the grain of conservative factions. It supports a greater level of privatization and personal choice than liberals would want to see. It also comes without the backing of any political party or organization. It comes without lobbyists.

Unfortunately, politics could stand in the way of moving this concept forward. As politicians get mired in the "fix-du jour," the extensive changes proposed may be too broad for any one political party to get their arms around. They will want to focus more on what's wrong with the concept than what it is right with it. They can pick apart any part that doesn't mesh with their political beliefs and take issue with it. However, once the concept is understood, it can withstand almost any logical argument. It can accommodate the many varied potential and perceived issues. But it will have to survive the politics, because politics will come.

It is my hope that public opinion and support would be the answer. Should a proposal such as this one be put on a national ballot, it could take the politics out of the equation. More importantly, if the public opinion and support gathered were enough to warrant debate and ultimate passage, our representatives would have to pay notice and abide by the public that put them in their offices.

With passage of this proposal, America would set the standard and become a model for all democracies on how social security should be organized and funded. Instead of admiring other countries' health plans, they will be looking to our all-encompassing program, which treats all Americans as equals in providing the necessary basic financial securities to all of its citizens.